Leckie✕Leckie
Scotland's leading educational publishers

CfE Higher
HISTORY
GRADE A BOOSTER

John Kerr

001/03042015

10 9 8 7 6 5 4 3 2 1

ISBN 9780007590865

Published by
Leckie & Leckie Ltd
An imprint of HarperCollins*Publishers*
Westerhill Road, Bishopbriggs, Glasgow, G64 2QT
T: 0844 576 8126   F: 0844 576 8131
leckieandleckie@harpercollins.co.uk
www.leckieandleckie.co.uk

Publisher: Katherine Wilkinson
Project manager: Craig Balfour

Special thanks to
Louise Robb (copy edit & proofread)
Felicity Kendal (proofread)
Keren McGill (proofread & editorial)
Jouve (layout)
Ink Tank (cover)

Printed in Italy by Grafica Veneta S.p.A

A CIP Catalogue record for this book is available from the British Library.

Acknowledgements
P2 © Shutterstock.com, P6 Topical Press Agency / Stringer / Getty Images; P16 Hulton Archive / Stringer / Getty Images; P46 Universal History Archive / Contributor / Getty Images; P64 Afro Newspaper/ Gado / Contributor / Getty Images

Contents

Introduction   3

Why should I buy this book?   3
How should I use this book?   3
What is in this book?   4

Chapter 1 – The Higher History Exam   7

Introduction to the exam   7
Sections 1–3   7
Time management   9
The extended responses   9
Beginning the exam   11

Chapter 2 – Section 1 of the Higher History Exam   15

Section 1 overview   15
The source evaluation question   19
The comparison question   28
The 'how fully' question   37

Chapter 3 – Sections 2 & 3 of the Higher History Exam 47

Sections 2 & 3 overview   47
Structure – the introduction   48
Structure – the conclusion   53
Knowledge marks   55
Analysis and evaluation marks   58

Chapter 4 – The History Assignment   65

What is the History Assignment?   65
What is the History Resource Sheet?   69
Summary   72

Introduction

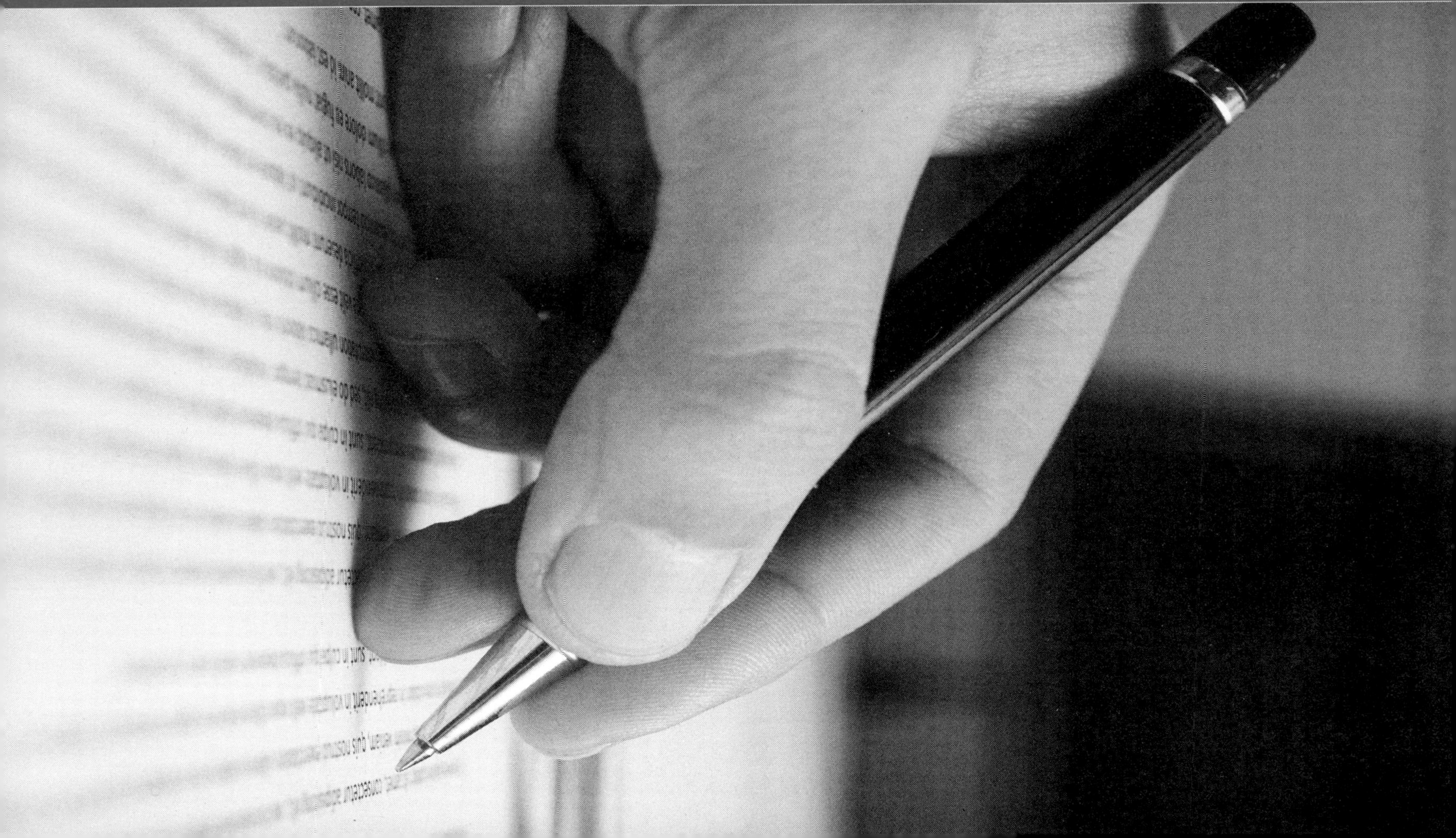

Introduction

Why should I buy this book?

The simple answer is because it will help you boost your grade. Whether you are trying to gain a basic pass at Higher or are aiming for an A, there is a wealth of information in this book that will help you to achieve your goals.

How do I know that is true?

The author is John Kerr. He has written books on every level of secondary history teaching, he is an examiner for the SQA and every year presents revision courses for hundreds of students across Scotland. On top of that, he teaches his own Higher classes as a high school teacher. He knows what you need to do to be successful and he presents it in a way that you will understand easily.

How should I use this book?

This book is **not** intended to be read all at once. In fact some parts may put you off if you tackle them too early, as they will deal with sections of the course you have not yet started. However, when you are working on the History Assignment or checking how to write extended responses or how to prepare answers to source-based questions, then turn to the relevant section and use it to help you get the best possible results.

Will this book tell me all the facts I need for the exam?

This book will **not** tell you all the topic facts needed for your Higher History course. Course content facts and tips can be found in the Leckie & Leckie book *Higher History Success Guide* by John Kerr.

Finally, be careful when speaking to people who sat their Higher History before 2014. The course and the exam have changed. From 2014 onwards, your Higher History exam paper will look completely different from any earlier Higher History exam paper. Beware of using earlier past papers; they will not be accurate in their layout.

What is in this book?

Chapter 1	The Higher History exam	A general overview of the whole exam.
Chapter 2	Section 1 of the exam paper	How to develop the different skills you need to deal with the three different types of questions you will be asked in Section 1 (Scottish).
Chapter 3	Sections 2 & 3 of the exam paper	In these sections of the exam you will be asked to write two extended responses, one from Section 2 (Britain) and one from Section 3 (Europe and the World). The chapter is divided into topics including: how best to write an introduction, using your knowledge appropriately, the meaning of analysis and evaluation, and guidance about writing conclusions. The chapter ends with advice about how your extended responses will be marked.
Chapter 4	The History Assignment	You will write a History Assignment a few weeks before the main exam. It is worth 30 marks out of a total of 90. The guidance offered in this chapter will give you the best possible start towards gaining a very good grade at Higher History.

The Higher History Exam

Introduction to the exam

Your exam booklet is divided into three main Historical Study sections:

- Scottish History
- British History
- European/World History

In Section 1 you must answer three questions based on four sources from Scottish history. In Section 2 you must write one extended response, also known as an essay, based on the British topic you have learned about. In Section 3 you must write another essay based on the European or World topic or topics you have learned about.

Sections 1–3

What is in Section 1?

Section 1 will contain sets of questions and sources on five Scottish-based topics:

- The Wars of Independence, 1249–1328
- The Age of the Reformation, 1542–1603
- The Treaty of Union, 1689–1740
- Migration and Empire, 1830–1939
- The Impact of the Great War, 1914–28

You will have studied **one** of those topics. Each topic has three questions based on four sources. You must answer all of the questions in your chosen topic. In total this section is worth **20 marks**.

What is in Section 2?

Section 2 will contain sets of questions based on five British History topics:

- Part One: Church, State and Feudal Society, 1066–1406
- Part Two: The Century of Revolutions, 1603–1702
- Part Three: The Atlantic Slave Trade
- Part Four: Britain, 1851–1951
- Part Five: Britain and Ireland, 1900–85

You will have studied **one** of those topics. Each topic has three questions. You must choose one of the questions to write an extended response worth **20 marks**.

What is in Section 3?

Section 3 will contain sets of questions based on nine Europe and World History topics:

- Part One: The Crusades, 1071–1204
- Part Two: The American Revolution, 1763–87
- Part Three: The French Revolution, to 1799
- Part Four: Germany, 1815–1939
- Part Five: Italy, 1815–1939
- Part Six: Russia, 1881–1921
- Part Seven: USA, 1918–68
- Part Eight: Appeasement and the Road to War, 1919–39
- Part Nine: The Cold War, 1945–89

You will have studied **one** of those topics. Each topic has three questions. You must choose one of the questions to write an extended response worth **20 marks**.

Time management

How much time do I have to complete the exam paper?

The Higher History examination lasts for 2 hours 20 minutes (140 minutes). In that time you must write answers to all three sections. To be successful you must organise your time and that means doing some maths! The total marks for the paper is 60. So a simple division of time would suggest that you have about 2.5 minutes per mark.

Is it that simple?

Not really, because you have to think about time you will spend reading the questions, making choices and in Section 1 you will have four sources to read carefully. So if you allow 20 minutes just for reading and thinking, you will still have 2 hours to write your answers. Remember you can write your answers in any order (Section 1 doesn't have to be done first), so you could start with the extended responses first.

The extended responses

Should I do two extended responses from the same section (especially if I don't see any questions I want to answer in the other section)?

No! Never do two extended responses from the same section. In other words **never** do two extended responses on the British topic or from the European and World topic. If you do, both extended responses will be marked but only the extended response with the best mark will be counted. The other extended response will get 0 marks, no matter how good it is.

If I spend too long on the first extended response should I still try to do a second extended response?

First of all **do not** spend too long on one extended response. You **must** be disciplined about time. Allow about 1 hour to do Section 1 (even if you do Section 1 later). Then you can use 40 minutes on each extended response. Remember, time taken over 40 minutes is really time being stolen from your other answers.

Think about this: if you have written quite a good first extended response you might get 14 out of 20 marks after 40 minutes writing. By writing for more than 40 minutes (and stealing time from your other extended response) you might push it up to 17 out of 20. That means you have gained 3 marks by overshooting time.

Unless your second extended response is completely and utterly wrong, or is irrelevant or only lasts a few lines, you are still guaranteed to get more than 3. If your second extended response even slightly tries to answer the question – even if there are errors and some of it is irrelevant – you will still get about 7 or 8 marks. So, with the example here, 14 marks plus 8 equals 22 marks – and that's a pass (i.e. is more than 20 out of 40).

By only doing one extended response, even one that is a very good A pass, you will only get 17/40 – a poor fail. So remember this rule: organise your time and make sure you do what you need to do to complete the exam.

What will the extended response questions be like?

All extended responses are a similar style. You will never get a 'tell a story' extended response that asks you only to 'describe'. In the Higher History exam you will always be asked whether or not you agree with a particular point of view or you will be asked to judge the success of something. Here are some examples:

From 'Church, State and Feudal Society, 1066–1406'	To what extent was the Black Death responsible for the decline of the feudal system?
From 'The Century of Revolutions, 1603–1702'	'Charles I's attempt to impose his authority in Scotland was a failure.' How valid is this view?
From 'Britain, 1851–1951'	How important was the influence of municipal socialism in persuading the Liberal Government to introduce social reforms between 1906 and 1914?
From 'Germany, 1815–1939'	How important were cultural factors in the growth of national feeling in Germany between 1815 and 1850?

From 'USA, 1918–1968'	How successful was the New Deal in solving the social and economic problems of the USA in the 1930s?
From 'Appeasement and the Road to War, to 1939'	To what extent was the outbreak of war in September 1939 brought about by the developing crisis in Poland?

Are there 'must remember' rules about writing extended responses?

Yes. The single most important piece of advice to any candidate is to read the question carefully and ask yourself these two questions:

- What **topic** is this question about?
- What do I have to **do** to answer the question successfully?

The SQA has reported that if candidates read each question carefully and work out what that question is asking them to do, it would make a massive contribution to raising standards of performance. Every year markers find a significant number of extended responses written by candidates who seem to have a prepared answer in their heads and use it regardless of the exact wording in the real exam question. The reason for this is that candidates presumably hoped for different questions and failed to adapt their answers. Don't be one of these candidates.

Beginning the exam

What should I do first when I open my exam question booklet?

You will be nervous and adrenaline will be pumping but breathe deeply and think carefully. You will want to get started quickly, but take your time and do not rush. Scan through the questions and make sure you are looking at the questions in the section of the course you have studied. Look for questions you might want to answer.

Make sure you have understood not only what the question is **about** but also what you have to **do**. In other words, see what the topic is but also what the task is asking you to do. For example, here is a question about the Liberal reforms in the 'Britain, 1851–1951' topic:

'To what extent was fear over national security a major factor leading to the Liberal reforms of 1906–1914?'

This question is really asking about **why** the reforms happened, but students often see the words 'Liberal reforms 1906–1914' and start writing about the Liberal Reforms themselves. Such an answer that ignores the question about why they happened, is therefore irrelevant and would not score highly.

Finally, read all the questions again in your chosen topic and make sure you answer the question that you are asked.

Chapter 2 – Section 1 of the Higher History Exam

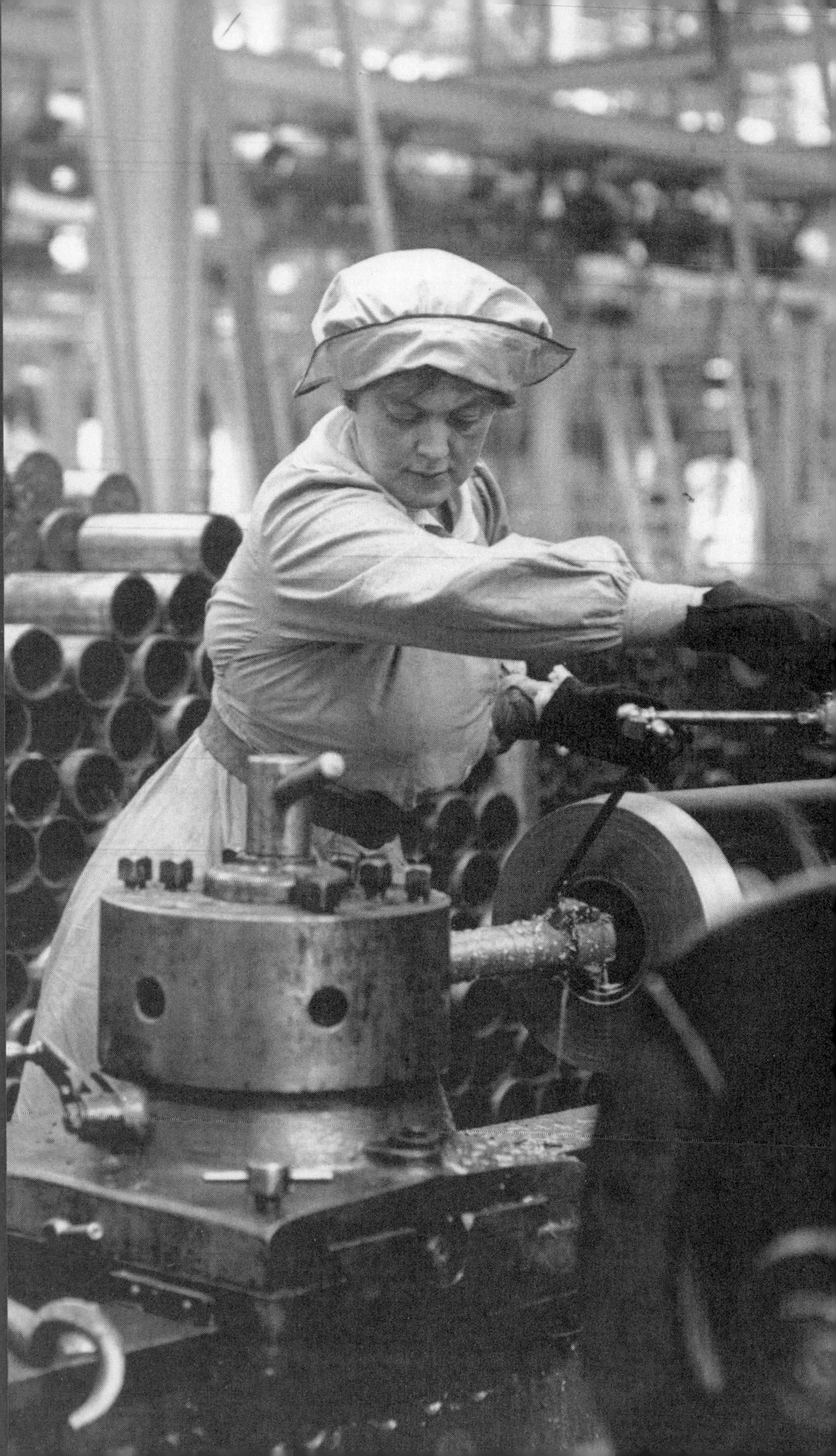

Section 1 of the Higher History Exam

Section 1 overview

What do I have to do in Section 1?

You will have four sources to use and **three questions** to answer. You must work out how much time you should spend on each question. You do not have to do Section 1 first – you may prefer to get the extended response questions in Sections 2 and 3 out of the way first.

Do I have to choose which topic to answer?

No – the choice will have been made by your teacher/tutor, who will have made the decision about which topic you study. You need to make sure that you answer questions on the topic you have been taught.

How do I know what the content is of each Section 1 topic?

Put simply, the content is what you have been learning about in class. More precisely, your topic syllabus is divided into four main areas of mandatory content (mandatory being the content that you must know about). You can look them up yourself if you wish on the SQA website at http://www.sqa.org.uk/files_ccc/ CfE_CourseUnitSupportNotes_Higher_SocialStudies_History.pdf

Here is an example for 'The Impact of the Great War, 1914–28':

Mandatory content	Illustrative areas
1. Scots on the Western Front	Scotland on the eve of the Great War: political, social and economic conditions; martial traditions; voluntary recruitment; the experience of Scots on the Western Front, with reference to the battles of Loos and the Somme; the kilted regiments; the role of Scottish military personnel in terms of commitment, casualties, leadership and overall contribution to the military effort.
2. Domestic impact of war: society and culture	Recruitment and conscription; pacifism and conscientious objection; DORA; changing role of women in wartime, including rent strikes; scale and effects of military losses on Scottish society; commemoration and remembrance.
3. Domestic impact of war: industry and economy	Wartime effects of war on industry, agriculture and fishing; price rises and rationing; post-war economic change and difficulties; post-war emigration; the land issue in the Highlands and Islands.
4. Domestic impact of war: politics	The impact of the war on political developments as exemplified by the growth of radicalism, the ILP and Red Clydeside, continuing support for political unionism and the crisis of Scottish identity. The significance of the Great War in the development of Scottish identity.

How many marks is Section 1 worth?

Section 1 is worth a total of **20 marks**. Each of the three questions has its own number of marks indicated after the question.

How long do I have to answer Section 1?

The whole exam lasts for 2 hours and 20 minutes. There are no breaks between Sections 1, 2 and 3. Elsewhere in this book it was suggested that your two extended responses should take 40 minutes each, that is 1 hour 20 minutes in total. That means you should aim to do the three questions in Section 1 within one hour.

Will the different styles of questions always be in the same order, year after year?

No. For example, an evaluation question might appear as question 1 in one year, then be the last question the following year. The only thing that will stay the same is the number of marks the questions are worth.

Will there be a question on each part of the syllabus?

No, although each topic has four areas of mandatory content, there are only three questions in Section 1. So, each year, one area of mandatory content in the course will be left out of the exam.

Should I skip a question if I am unsure of the answer?

Only if you really can write nothing in response to the question. If you write nothing, the only thing a marker can do is to give you nothing. Markers will give you marks even if you have not directly answered the question. If you can select relevant extracts from the source and even give a very simple answer then you will quite probably get at least a few marks. Give a marker the chance to give you marks!

What types of questions will I be asked in Section 1?

There are **three** different types of question, with each one testing different source handling skills.

Source evaluation questions

These are worth **6 marks** and will usually be identified with a question asking, 'Evaluate the usefulness of Source ... as evidence of ...'. In this type of question you are being asked to judge how useful the source is as a piece of evidence giving us historical information.

Comparison questions

These are worth **5 marks** and will ask you to compare two points of view overall and in detail. The wording of the question could be something like, 'Compare the views of Sources C and D about ...'.

'How fully' questions

These are worth **9 marks** and will ask about a whole section of the mandatory content. Remember there are four of these sections for each topic. You could be asked, 'How fully does Source ... illustrate the impact of the war on the Scottish economy between 1914 and 1928'. This question relates to the mandatory content section 'Domestic impact of war: industry and economy' in the topic 'The Impact of the Great War, 1914–1928'. In this type of question you have to identify which parts of the source content give information relevant to the question. The source will never provide all the necessary information. You are also expected to state that the source **partly** answers the question, but then you must include information from your own knowledge to provide an answer that gives a fuller picture in terms of the question.

How many sources will there be in my exam paper?

There will be **four sources** to read and questions will follow, based on them. There will always be a mix of primary and secondary sources.

Why are we given sources in the exam?

Sources are the raw materials of history. Historians need skills of analysis, and to be successful in Higher History, you are expected to be able to use these analysing skills to reach balanced answers to questions using the available evidence, both from the sources provided and from your own knowledge.

The source evaluation question

How will the source evaluation question be marked?

The source evaluation question is worth **6 marks**, broken down as follows:

- **Origin and possible purpose – up to 4 marks**
- **Content of the source – up to 2 marks**
- **Your own knowledge – up to 2 marks**

It will ask something like, 'Evaluate the usefulness of ... as evidence of ...'. This question will always feature a primary source only. There will be no picture sources to evaluate. Below the question you will see some helpful guidance on how to answer the question, as follows:

In making a judgement you should refer to:

- *The origin and possible purpose of the source*
- *The content of the source*
- *Your own knowledge*

How do I get marks for writing about 'origin' and 'possible purpose' of the source?

The 'origin' means the author of the source. Above the source you will find information about its provenance. That means where the source comes from. You will also be given the name of the author – but remember it is not enough just to copy out who the author was. Sources are chosen by examiners so that the information given about the author will provide you with an opportunity to comment on what it is about that information that helps to make the source useful.

If you simply state who the author is, what the title of the source is and when it was published then you are unlikely to get any 'origin' marks. For example, if you were given an extract from the 'Lubeck Letter', an important document from the time of the Scottish Wars of Independence, and you simply wrote that the letter was from William Wallace and Andrew Moray and sent to merchants across the North Sea, then you will get no marks because you have not made any attempt to explain its importance. A better answer would be, 'this letter was written by Wallace and Moray, joint Guardians of Scotland, and this is very useful because it shows their awareness of what was needed politically and economically to help Scotland fight against Edward'.

What does 'possible purpose' mean?

It means why we think the source was written. Some sources are obvious. An official regimental history is to record for future historians the details of a regiment at a certain time. However, a letter or a memoir is more difficult. Was it written to boast about something or to inform relatives? The point about 'possible purpose' is for you to make a sensible judgement about why it was written and why that makes it useful to historians. Remember that biased sources are also useful because they show the feelings people had at the time. Letters and diaries are personal and are useful because they show the thoughts of people at the time.

Does it matter what type of source it is?

Yes. Extra marks can be gained by commenting on the type of source. You must also state the advantages and disadvantages of such a source in terms of its usefulness as evidence. For example a diary entry or a letter would be useful for showing a personal point of view but might also lack exact details. On the other hand, an official war record or official history of a regiment would be researched, detailed and accurate. A memoir may also be accurate, but this is not guaranteed as it would be based only on someone's memory.

A medieval chronicle about the Scottish Wars of Independence would be useful as a record of what was known at the time, but would also be biased depending on whether it was a Scottish or English chronicle. Daniel Defoe's writings about the state of Scotland before the Union would give a detailed picture of how people felt about the proposed Union, but it would also be biased because he was an English spy. So you should always think about what type of source it is and what that tells us about the reliability of the source as accurate evidence.

Does the date of the source matter?

Marks are available for commenting on when the source was produced (you will be given a date for the source). Is it first-hand evidence just before something happened? Was it produced while important events were happening and will show how people felt? Or was it produced after the events on which it is commenting and so the writer can be 'wise after the event' (historians call this hindsight)?

How do I get marks for writing about the content of the source?

There are up to **2 marks** for referring to the content of the source. You may quote sections from the source, but make sure your selection is relevant to the question **and** that you explain clearly why the extract you have quoted makes the source useful as evidence in terms of the question.

How do I get marks for using my own knowledge?

You will also gain up to **2 marks** for recall. That means you must show off your own knowledge, as long as it is relevant and accurate. You can get recall marks anywhere in the answer to this question. If you use your own knowledge (that is, not from information provided anywhere in the source) to explain a point you are making about origin or purpose or content then that counts as recall. However, to be sure, a good way to include recall is to mention information that is not present in the source, but if it had been present then it would have made the source more useful as evidence about an event. Here you can show off what you know about a subject, but remember to answer in terms of the question. If you are asked to evaluate a source as evidence of the battle of Loos, there is no point writing about recruitment and why so many young men joined the army. Your information might be correct but it is not relevant.

Must I always evaluate using my own knowledge as well as the source?

Yes. In this sort of question recalled knowledge is vital. In example question 1 below for instance, it is impossible to judge the usefulness of a source about the experience of Scottish soldiers on the Western Front without knowing what conditions on the Western Front were like.

Marking summary

For an evaluation question that asks, 'Evaluate the usefulness of Source X as evidence of ...' , there are **6 marks** in total:

- Up to 4 marks for commenting on the author, the time it was produced, the type of source it is and the purpose.
- Up to 2 marks for selecting extracts from the source content and explaining why they make the source useful as evidence for finding out about the focus of the question.
- You can also get up to 2 marks for including your own relevant information that is not in the source, but would make the source more useful as evidence in terms of the question if it had been included.

Are there common errors I should avoid?

Yes, there are two mistakes often made by candidates. The first is not answering in terms of the question and the second common error is 'listing'.

What does 'in terms of the question' mean?
Your answer must be relevant to the question asked. In a question that asks you to evaluate the usefulness of ..., you must judge its use in helping to answer the question set. For example, if the question asked about the importance of William Wallace to the Scots' resistance against Edward, you would not get extra knowledge marks for information about Robert the Bruce. Your information about Bruce might be perfectly correct but it would have nothing to do with the question, which is about William Wallace. Always check what the question is asking you to do. An evaluation question will always ask you to judge the usefulness of a source as evidence about something. It's the 'something' that is important as the focus for your answer.

What is listing?
Listing means writing information that may be correct and even relevant but you make no attempt to explain how each point made links to the question. There are no marks for just copying chunks of the source. Even if you select sections from the sources that are relevant to the question you will still only

get **one mark in total** for this section, because you have not explained how the sources are relevant to the question. For two marks you must mention two points from the source and **also** explain why the evidence you have selected is relevant to the question.

Example 1

Here is an example of a source evaluation question from 'The Impact of the Great War, 1914–28'.

Source A is from a letter written by Private Douglas Hepburn of the London Scottish to his parents in October 1915.

My dear mum and dad,
We have been in the trenches for ten days and had a very rough time of it coming out with only 160 men left in our battalion. The Germans at the point where we attacked were ready and too strong for us. As we rushed up to the edge the machine gun was turned on us and we suffered high casualties. In the morning we came back and the sight of the field was rotten. It was a typical battlefield – see all the dead bodies lying about in different positions, all our own men of course, especially just in front of the German's barbed wire. To see thousands of our troops, stretching right across the plain to the horizon, and stretcher-bearers going here and there, doing their work and the wounded crying for the bearers. It was a sight that could not easily be forgotten on that grey, misty and damp morning.

Evaluate the usefulness of **Source A** as evidence of the experience of Scottish soldiers on the Western Front. (**6 marks**)

In making a judgement you should refer to:

- *the origin and possible purpose of the source*
- *the content of the source*
- *your own knowledge*

Example of a weak answer

A | *The source is useful because it gives a description of a trench battle. It says they have lost a lot of men – 'coming out with only 160 men in our battalion'. It also says that, 'The Germans at the point where we attacked were ready and too strong for us' and, 'in front of the German's barbed wire'. The source is also useful because it shows that soldiers were upset by all the deaths – 'It was a sight that could not easily be forgotten'.*

Why is this a weak answer, and how would it be marked?

This answer is weak mainly because:

1. The answer fails to evaluate by referring to the origins and possible purpose of the source. (0 marks)
2. The answer mainly copies phrases from the source. (1 mark)
3. The answer contains no recalled knowledge. (0 marks)
4. There is no attempt to provide a balanced answer, suggesting the source might have its limits as a useful piece of evidence.

It would gain a maximum of **1 mark out of 6**.

Example of a much better answer

A | *This source is partly useful for finding out about the experience of Scottish soldiers on the Western Front but it has limits. The letter is from a soldier on the Western Front – an eyewitness who experienced what he describes, making the source very useful.*

The purpose is to let his parents know how he is getting on and what his experiences are like. This makes the source very useful as primary evidence giving first-hand detail. As it is a letter to his parents the writer is likely to tell the truth but maybe not include details that would worry his parents. Letters were often censored but this one seems to have got past the censor.

The detail given matches up with what I know. In trench warfare defence was usually stronger than attack and barbed wire and machine guns usually caused the high casualties mentioned in the source. The letter mentions the stronger German position and that was also usually true. The Germans chose to dig trenches on slightly higher ground where they could see an attack coming.

The source does however have limits. It gives no information about the experience of soldiers in the trenches such as the lice, the food, the boredom or the fear. There is also information missing about the experience of heavy artillery barrages and even gas attacks.

Overall the source is quite useful for giving an impression, but many more letters would be needed to gain a full picture of the experience of Scottish soldiers on the Western Front.

Why is this a much better answer, and how would it be marked?
It is a better answer, and one that will gain full marks, because:

1. It not only identifies the origin and purpose of the source but also explains why each makes it a useful source. (2 marks)
2. It provides detail of trench warfare that matches other reports and does make clear how the evidence selected is relevant to the question. (2 marks)
3. It includes detailed recalled information. It also provides a balanced evaluation of the usefulness of the source and includes more recall that helps evaluate the evidence in terms of the question asked. (2 marks)

It would gain the full **6 marks out of 6**.

Example 2

Here is an example of a source evaluation question from 'The Wars of Independence, 1249–1328'.

Source B is a letter from Andrew Moray and William Wallace to the merchants of Lubeck, October 1297.

'Andrew of Moray and William Wallace, leaders of the army of the kingdom of Scotland, and of the community of the realm, to their wise and discreet beloved friends the mayors and common people of Lubeck and of Hamburg, greetings and increasing sincere affection. We have been told by trustworthy merchants of the kingdom of Scotland that you are considerate, helpful and well disposed in all cases and matters affecting us and our merchants and we are therefore more obliged to give you our thanks and a worthy repayment: to this end we willingly enter into an undertaking with you, asking you to have it announced to your merchants that they can have safe access to all ports of the Scottish kingdom with their merchandise, because the kingdom of Scotland, thanks be to God, has been recovered by war from the power of the English.

Fare well.'

Given at Haddington in Scotland, 11 October 1297.

Q Evaluate the usefulness of **Source B** as evidence of the importance of William Wallace to Scottish resistance against the English. (**6 marks**)

In making a judgement you should refer to:

- *the origin and possible purpose of the source*
- *the content of the source*
- *your own knowledge*

Example of a weak answer

A William Wallace was important because he was a leader of Scotland who defeated the English. He fought with Andrew Moray who was another leader. The letter is useful because it shows that Wallace wants Scotland to trade with Lubeck and Hamburg to help Scotland recover from the wars with England. The letter also shows that Wallace thinks that Scotland has been freed from the English.

Why is this a weak answer, and how would it be marked?

1. It has a factually weak beginning. It claims Wallace was a leader of Scotland but the letter only claims that Wallace and Moray were leaders of the army of Scotland. (0 marks)
2. This answer only outlines the very basic premise of the letter. (1 mark)
3. There is no attempt to evaluate the origin and purpose of the letter. (0 marks)
4. There is almost no recall or development of any point raised in the letter. (0 marks)

This is a weak answer that only gains **1 mark out of 6** for the use of content to link Wallace with Scottish economic recovery.

Example of a much better answer

The source is partly useful in telling us about the importance of William Wallace to the Scottish resistance against the English. This letter is one of the few pieces of primary evidence we have about Wallace. It was written after the Battle of Stirling Bridge and is an attempt to tell important trading partners that Scotland was 'open for business' after 'being recovered by war from the power of the English'. Lubeck and Hamburg were important north German trading ports and Scotland needed resources such as timber from there. The source is therefore useful in showing how Wallace was more than a fighting warrior because the letter is trying to make friends with the German merchants by calling them 'considerate, helpful and well disposed'.

Scotland needed to trade and assure foreign traders they were safe in Scotland. Many traders had been hurt by Edward's invasion of Scotland, especially the destruction of Berwick. The letter is also useful in that it shows Wallace sharing leadership of the army with Andrew Moray. It also refers to the Community of the Realm. After Stirling Bridge, Wallace and Moray were made Guardians of Scotland by the Community of the Realm and in that role Wallace was trying to build up Scotland's strength. The Community of the Realm was made up of the important church figures and nobles of Scotland and their recognition of Wallace as Guardian shows his importance as a recognised leader in resisting the English.

Why is this a much better answer, and how would it be marked?
It is a better answer, and one that will gain the **full 6 marks**, because:

1. The answer deals with the origin and purpose of the letter. (2 marks)
2. The answer develops at least four points from the source and explains their significance. (2 marks)
3. There are at least four main pieces of recall used to develop the answer. (2 marks)

The comparison question

How will the comparison question be marked?

The comparison question is worth a maximum of **5 marks**, broken down as follows:

- **Overall comparison – up to 2 marks**
- **Detailed comparisons – up to 4 marks**

A comparison question requires you to make clear connections between sources. The skill being assessed is your ability to compare and that does not mean your ability to describe two sources. You must be able to show the similarities and differences between the sources. You will always get a comparison question in your Higher History exam and it will be worth 5 marks.

How do I answer a comparison question?

You must compare the sources overall and in detail. These two processes can be done in any order.

You must make **an overall comparison**, which can be worth **up to 2 marks**:

- You will get **1 mark** for describing the main points made by the first source and then deciding if the second source says much the same sort of thing or if it takes a different point of view.

- You will get an **extra 'overall' mark** if you develop your overall comparison. This means that rather than just writing that the sources agree or disagree on a general point, be more specific about the points they agree or disagree on.

You must compare the sources **in detail**:

- You can get **up to 4 marks** for comparing the sources in detail. You will get **1 mark** for each detailed comparison you make.
- To get a comparison mark you must find a point in each source that the sources agree or disagree on. When you have written down what point they agree or disagree about you **must** back up your point by quoting from each source. Your quotes must clearly concern the point you say they agree or disagree about.
- It is **not enough** just to list points of difference between the sources. In fact you might get **no marks** for simply stating, 'Source A says … but B says …'
- To ensure you get the 4 marks available for detailed comparison you should write about four different points of comparison.
- You will get no marks for stating, 'Source B thinks … but source C does not mention that point at all'. This is called a ghost comparison and because there is no comparison here, you will get **no marks**.

Here is an example of a comparison answer dealing with the battle of Stirling Bridge from the unit 'The Wars of Independence, 1249–1328'.

> *Sources A and B agree that Cressingham was killed and skinned by the Scots after the battle. Source A says, 'Cressingham, a leader amongst the English knights, was killed during the battle and later skinned'. Source B agrees when it says, 'the treacherer Cressingham was skinned following his death during the battle'.*

You will get 1 mark for making this comparison because you have stated the point of comparison and then supported it by making a detailed, quoted, reference to each source.

Should I organise my answer around the words 'overall' and 'in detail'?

Yes, it makes it easy for a marker to give you marks by following the recommended style of answering. Start your answer with the word 'overall' and then identify the main difference between the sources. You should then use the phrase 'in detail' and then write the rest of your answer, comparing the sources point by point.

Take one point from the source and show how it is supported by, or disagrees with, the other source. Keep going to and fro between the sources until you have finished comparing them. Remember it is not enough just to quote a sentence from one source then compare by quoting from another. By all means do that as part of your answer, but you should also explain the point being made by your extracts in your own words and use recall to develop your comparison. That is what is meant by a developed comparison.

Example 1

Here is an example of a comparison question from 'Migration and Empire, 1830–1939'.

Source A is from the report of the Education Commission (Scotland) (1866).

> The people in the Clyde district are of the poorest classes and this district has a large mixture of Irish immigrants. For this large Irish element and their needs there exists no school within the district, beyond a private adventure school in one of the wynds. Roman Catholic children are indeed to be found in the other schools but in comparatively small numbers and their attendance is extremely irregular. It is a fact that many children in the Clyde district, both Catholic and Protestant, but chiefly the former, attend no school. What are these neglected children doing then, if they are selling matches and running errands, cared for by no-one, not at school? They are idling in the streets and wynds, tumbling about in the gutters.

Source B is from W. Hamish Fraser and R. J. Morris (eds), *People and Society in Scotland Vol.II, 1830–1914* (1990).

The largest number of schools, pupils and teachers was to be found in Glasgow, but many of those were Catholic schools outside the state system. Irish settlement, especially after the Famine, produced an ever-growing demand for Catholic schools and teachers. Nonetheless, by the 1860s, the Catholic clergy could boast that they had overcome the immense difficulties and could offer pupils instruction in the three Rs and the Bible. But the community lacked the resources to pay adequate school fees or to raise the necessary funds towards teachers' salaries and school buildings. As a result, by the end of the century, there was a growing crisis in Catholic education.

Compare the views in **Sources A** and **B** about the provision of education for Irish immigrants to Scotland. (**5 marks**)

Compare the content overall and in detail.

Example of a weak answer

Sources A and B agree to an extent. Source A says there was very little education for Irish immigrants but source B says there was some but not enough. Source B says the Catholic priests did what they could to teach children reading and writing and the Bible. Source A says that not many Catholic children went to school but B says there were not enough Catholic schools to meet demand. Finally source A thinks that Catholic children did not want to go to school but source B thinks there were just not enough schools to meet demand.

Why is this a weak answer, and how would it be marked?

1. There is only a very vague attempt to introduce the answer with an overall comparison.

2. The writer simply picks out points from the sources and does not explain or develop the point being made.

At best this might get 1 mark for an overall comparison and 1 mark for listing (**2 marks out of 5** at best). Listing means you pick correct points from a source but do not explain their meaning in any way. In this case a sentence explaining the point being made by each comparison would have been enough to get more marks.

Example of a much better answer

A This is the overall comparison:

Overall, Source A suggests that the provision of education for Irish immigrants was almost non-existent and children of Irish immigrants did not want to attend schools. On the other hand source B suggests that the problem was one of supply to meet the demand of an immigrant population that did want a Catholic education.

This is detailed comparison number 1:

In detail source A states there was a lack of educational provision for Irish immigrants in the Clyde area. From 1840 onwards west central Scotland experienced a huge influx of Irish migrants as a result of the potato famine and poverty in Ireland and the Clyde area had few resources to cope with the huge increase in demand for many services, including schools ('For this large Irish element and their needs there exists no school within the district'). Source B on the other hand provides a more positive view about educational provision for Catholic Irish immigrants.

The Catholic Church made big efforts to look after the Irish migrants. 'The Catholic clergy … could offer pupils instruction in the three Rs and the Bible.' Partly the church wanted to prevent assimilation with Protestant Scotland but the Church also genuinely wanted to help their people with many social and religious activities to support the new incomers.

This is detailed comparison number 2:

Source A continues, stating that, 'Roman Catholic children are indeed to be found in the other schools but in comparatively small numbers', but source B claims that demand was high for education by writing, 'Irish settlement, especially after the Famine, produced an ever-growing demand for Catholic schools and teachers'. The point here is that there was a lot of prejudice and in some places Catholic Irish children were not welcomed in Church of Scotland schools. Also many Catholic families did not want their children going outside their Catholic world.

This is detailed comparison number 3:

Finally source A implies that Catholic children avoided school through choice and did not want education whereas source B suggests that the problem lay with the lack of resources and money to provide schools for growing demand. Demand for schools was so great that 'the community lacked the resources to pay adequate school fees or to raise the necessary funds towards teachers' salaries and school buildings'. The problem was not lack of attendance but lack of places to attend! Not until the 20th century did the state provide funds for basic education for all.

Why is this a much better answer, and how would it be marked?

1. The answer starts with an overall comparison that shows understanding of both sources. This gains 2 marks.
2. The answer then gives at least three direct comparisons.
3. The comparisons are relevant and connected to each other.
4. Recall is used (**but is not needed** in a comparison question) to explain attitudes or details mentioned in the extracts.
5. The answer contains comparisons of opinion but provides reasons for the differences.

This answer scored highly simply by following the marking scheme process and gains **5 out of 5**. Your answer does need to be exactly like this, but there are five marks so you **must** try to do an overall comparison followed by at least three direct developed comparisons, as this answer has tried to do.

Example 2

Here is an example of a comparison question from 'The Treaty of Union, 1689–1740'.

Source C is from a letter written to the Earl of Mar to his brother in 1711.

Most Scots seem to be weary of this mistake of Union, as are the English. One opinion held by our countrymen for relieving us of this hardship is to dissolve the Union through an Act of Parliament in the House of Lords. This would put us in the same place as we were before 1707. Nevertheless, if this was possible, the English would make the Hanoverian Succession permanent. So in such a circumstance we are placed, and I believe never were Scots in harder circumstances, with the economy likely to remain flat for decades. If we saw a possibility of getting free from Union without war we would have some comfort, but that, I'm afraid, is impossible.

Source D is from Michael Fry, *England, Scotland and the Treaty of Union.*

To Scots, the Union looked within a short time to have been a terrible mistake. Even the supporters of Union regretted what they had done. No economic boom followed for at least half a century; businesses closed down rather than opened up in the new British common market. The English delayed paying the promised Equivalent, which was money they did not have, and treated the Scots at Westminster with contempt. By 1713, Scottish politicians at Westminster felt driven to a dramatic demonstration of their discontent, agreeing to propose a dissolution of the Union in the House of Lords. This failed by only four votes. Within a couple of years, armed revolt against the Union would break out in Scotland and Mar, indeed, was the leader of the rising.

Q Compare the views of **Sources C** and **D** about the effects of Union to 1740.
(**5 marks**)

Compare the content overall and in detail.

Example of a weak answer

Overall the two sources show that people in Scotland did not like the Union and that it had been a mistake. Sources C and D agree that the Scottish economy was not going to be helped by Union and both sources think that the Union should be undone. The sources think that trying to break the Union would result in war between England and Scotland.

Why is this a weak answer and how would it be marked?

1. It is a rather short answer that hints at some correct comparisons but does not use source evidence to support the points clearly.
2. The 'overall' section does gain 1 mark for recognising that both sources thought the Union was a mistake.
3. The detail section is weak with poor direct comparisons. The answer mentions the weak economy but does not use source evidence to support the point.
4. The point about war is weak and does not fully understand the source, nor is there any supporting evidence from the sources.
5. The information mentioned in points 3 and 4 here would qualify as listing therefore gain 1 mark for detailed comparison.

In total this answer gains **2 marks out of 5**.

Example of a much better answer

This is the overall comparison:

Overall, both sources refer to the feeling that the Union was a mistake, Scotland gained little benefit from it and that the Union itself would be hard to break short of war.

(continued)

This is detailed comparison number 1:

In detail both sources indicate that the Union was seen by many as a mistake. Source C states, 'Scots seemed to be weary of this mistake of Union', while source D states, 'To Scots, the Union looked to have been a terrible mistake'.

This is detailed comparison number 2:

Next, Source C mentions that the economy was likely to be 'flat for decades' and source D says that Scotland would see no economic boom 'for at least half a century'. This means that the Scots, who had believed the Union would bring economic good times to Scotland, were disappointed.

This is detailed comparison number 3:

Scots hoped that the Union could be undone by attempting to 'dissolve the Union . . . in the House of Lords' according to Source C and 'Scots politicians . . . propose a dissolution of the Union in the House of Lords' according to Source D.

This is detailed comparison number 4:

Finally Source C, a primary source, realised that 'getting free from Union without war . . . is impossible' while Source D, a secondary source with hindsight, reports that 'armed revolt against the Union would break out in Scotland'.

Why is this a much better answer, and how would it be marked?

1. The answer starts with an overall comparison that shows understanding of both sources. This gains 1 mark.
2. The answer then gives four direct comparisons.
3. The core meaning of the source selections are explained.
4. Each comparison is supported with accurate and relevant direct quotes from the sources.

This answer gained **5 out of 5** simply by following the marking scheme process.

A final tip

It is possible that a question might ask, 'Compare the views of ...' and it might be that they do not agree completely or disagree completely. In a comparison question you can gain marks for identifying and explaining points where the sources agree **and also** where they disagree. Don't always assume there will be a neat balanced answer. Use your judgement.

The 'how fully' question

This is the question that asks about one of the areas of mandatory content within each topic of Section 1. It is worth a maximum of **9 marks** as follows:

- **Content from the source – up to 3 marks**
- **Your own knowledge – up to 7 marks**

Remember that this is a judgement question. In other words, if you do not clearly make a judgement and state that the source does not give a **full** description or explanation of an event then you can only get a **maximum of 2 marks**. Once again, a useful way to start an answer to this type of question is to say 'partly'. That gives a basic answer to the question, 'How fully...'. The source will provide relevant information within the text but will not give the whole picture. That allows you to include other information relevant to the answer from your own knowledge in order to provide a full answer.

There are two phases in any answer to this type of question:

1. You must select relevant points from the source and develop each point with recalled detailed knowledge. There are **3 marks** available for doing this.
2. You must then bring in your own knowledge to show that there are other points relevant to the answer that are not in the sources. This part is worth up to **7 marks**.

Will a source ever give a full account of something?

In this type of question you must decide by how much the source gives a **full** explanation or description of an event – and your decision is always easy! Here's why: the source will never, ever, give a totally full explanation or description because there would be no opportunity for you to show off your own knowledge. Think about it. There are 3 marks available for selecting relevant material from the source and 7 more marks available for using your own knowledge to explain points not included in the source. If the source gave the whole story then how could you gain 7 marks? Therefore, your answer should always start by stating something like, 'The source **partly** explains/describes …'.

How do I make sure I gain the 3 marks for using the source?

You must use the source provided by finding three relevant points in the source, quoting them in your answer **and** explaining the point being made by your chosen quote. For example, in the section 'Migration and Empire, 1830–1939', if you had a question that asked how fully a source explained the reasons for Scots emigrating to other parts of the world, you would need to find three different reasons for Scottish migration within the source you are given and explain the meaning of the source extracts chosen.

How do I make sure I gain 7 marks for using my own knowledge?

You can get up to 7 marks for including as much accurate and relevant information from your own knowledge as you can. Your information should be relevant to the question. This means you should mention information which, if it had been included in the source, would have made it a much fuller answer. What you argue is that the source at present does not give the full picture of an event because important things have been left out. It is your job to mention the things that should be included in the source.

Remember: do not list! In a 'how fully' question listing can be disastrous because you will only get 1 mark out of 7. Think back to the 'Migration and Empire' question mentioned above about why Scots emigrated. If you simply write a list of events and people to do with Scots emigration or you just bullet point events such as 'Highland Clearances' or 'Emigration Societies' you will only get a **total of 1 mark for listing**. You **must** make it clear to a marker how your information is relevant to the question asked.

Example 1

Here is an example of a 'how fully' question, and some answers, from 'The Wars of Independence, 1249–1328'.

Source A is from a letter issued by King John at Kincardine or Brechin, July 1296.

In view of the fact that through bad and wrong advice and our own foolishness we have in many ways gravely displeased and angered our lord Edward by the grace of God King of England, in that while we still owed him fealty and homage we made an alliance with the King of France against him . . . we have defied our lord the King of England and have withdrawn ourselves from his homage and fealty by renouncing our homage . . . we have sent our men into his land of England to burn, loot, murder and commit other wrongs and have fortified the land of Scotland against him . . . for all these reasons the King of England entered the realm of Scotland and conquered it by force despite the army we sent against him, something he had a right to do as lord of his fee.

Therefore acting of our own free will we have surrendered the land of Scotland and all its people with the homage of them all to him.

How fully does **Source A** explain the relationship between John Balliol and Edward I? **(9 marks)**

Use the source and your own knowledge.

Example of a weak answer

When this source was written Scotland was at war with England. Balliol was Scottish king and he had promised to be loyal to Edward. This was called 'fealty' and Balliol had done homage for the throne of Scotland. Balliol had promised to support Edward but had broken his promise by signing an alliance with France against Edward of England.

(continued)

This source shows that the Scots had angered Edward by attacking England and Edward had invaded Scotland. The Scots were defeated at Dunbar and Edward chased Balliol across Scotland. This source shows that Balliol and the Scots have surrendered to Edward. The relationship between Balliol and Edward is that Balliol is now defeated and in danger of losing his crown.

Why is this a weak answer, and how would it be marked?

1. The answer really only describes what is in the source. There is a vague understanding of fealty and homage but it is not clear.
2. There is no context outlining the wider relationship between Balliol and Edward or between Scotland and England.
3. There is almost no analysis of the 'tone' of the source, which seems to suggest that Balliol had got himself into a mess as a result of bad advice and his own foolishness, and that Balliol has decided to surrender Scotland to Edward as a result of Balliol's own free will. In reality Balliol had been chased across Scotland and was captured. He had no choice – and certainly no 'free will'!
4. In essence this answer focuses on only one part of the relationship between Balliol and Edward. There should be much more.

The first part of the answer might gain 2 of the 3 available marks. It acknowledges that the war between Scotland and England came about by Balliol breaking his feudal promises. There is some explanation of what those promises involved.

Except for the already credited information about fealty and homage there is very little recall, apart from mentions of defeat at Dunbar, Edward invading and then chasing Balliol across Scotland. At best this would get 2 of the 7 available marks.

In total this answer would gain **4 out of 9 marks**, a generous mark given the shallowness of the answer.

Example of a much better answer

This source only partly shows the relationship between Edward and Balliol. It deals with the war between Scotland and England prompted by the Scots alliance with France and the attack into northern England, which 'displeased and angered our lord Edward'. Edward then launched an invasion starting at Berwick where the town was sacked. After that the Scots were defeated at Dunbar. Edward then went north, chasing the Scots. Balliol was eventually captured and his badges of office stripped from his coat, hence Balliol's nickname of 'toom tabard'. Scotland was then taken over by Edward.

On the other hand, the source does not fully explain the relationship between Balliol and Edward or the feudal agreements that existed between them. Nor does the source mention how Edward chose Balliol as king of Scotland.

The Great Cause was the question of who should rule Scotland after the death of Alexander III. Balliol was one of several 'competitors' and Edward was asked to judge the competing claims. Balliol was chosen mainly because he was closest in succession to Alexander.

Balliol did homage for Scotland and as such accepted Edward as his feudal overlord ('our lord Edward') and superior. By doing this, Balliol guaranteed to support Edward when called upon to do so. When Edward asked for help against the French, Balliol broke his oath of fealty by 'renouncing our homage'.

The relationship that had been agreed, of feudal vassal and overlord, had therefore been broken. Balliol's leadership of the Scottish army was weak and although the letter suggests that Balliol was surrendering Scotland of his own free will, the truth is that the Scots were defeated and Balliol had no choice. Edward had asserted his power and indeed his right to teach his vassal a lesson.

This source tries to sound as if Balliol has been foolish and is almost apologetic to Edward. The English invasion is described as, 'something he had a right to do as lord of his fee' and Scottish actions are described as the result of, 'bad and wrong advice and our own foolishness'.

Given that the source was written at or near the place that Balliol was captured, then it seems as if either Balliol was told to write this or he was making a last attempt to appease Edward.

Why is this a much better answer, and how would it be marked?

1. It sets context and explains the wider relationship between Edward and Balliol.

2. Appropriate vocabulary such as 'vassal' and 'overlord' is used.

3. The answer is an appropriate length.

4. There is good analysis of the content of the source.

5. There is a great deal of accurate and relevant detail.

6. Overall, this answer does try to evaluate how fully the source shows the relationship between Edward and Balliol.

This answer could easily gain 3 marks for developing the source and could also gain 5 out of 7 marks for some very specific points of recall. The minimum this answer would get would be **8 out of 9**.

Example 2

Here is an example of a 'how fully' question, and some answers, from 'The Age of Reformation, 1542–1603'.

Source A is from A. Ryrie, *The Origins of the Scottish Reformation*.

Radicalised Protestants gained confidence as they found remarkably few of their countrymen were willing to oppose them. Their cause was also aided by Scottish Catholicism's ability to rally support being considerably weakened by a decade-long period of public debate. It was no longer clear there was a banner to rally to within the Catholic Church in Scotland. Moreover, the events of the 1550s had left some Scots uncertain of trusting the French. This again led to many Scots looking to radicalised Protestants for direction. Critical in gaining support towards Reformation was the Protestant English being viewed as allies, rather than an enemy with imperial ambitions.

How fully does **Source A** explain the reasons for the Reformation of 1560? **(9 marks)**

Use the source and your own knowledge.

Example of a weak answer

The radical Protestants were confident because the ordinary people did not try to stop them. Another reason is that no reforms had happened in the Catholic Church and it was unable to stop the radical Protestants. People in Scotland also did not trust the Catholic French so they supported the Protestants and they also liked having Protestant England nearby in case they needed help.

Why is this a weak answer and how would it be marked?

1. It is very short and does not explain its points well.
2. Its main problem is that it only uses information in the source and makes no attempt to make a judgement about how fully the source explains reasons for the Reformation of 1560.

Answers which refer only to the source content and make no judgement can only be given 2 marks so this answer will get only **2 out of a possible 9 marks**.

Example of a much better answer

A Source A only partly explains the reasons for the Reformation of 1560. Firstly, the source says, 'Radicalised Protestants gained confidence as they found remarkably few of their countrymen were willing to oppose them'. This means that if Scots had tried to stop the Protestants then the Reformation would not have happened so quickly, but without opposition the radical Protestants could spread their ideas more easily.

Secondly, support for the Catholic Church was 'considerably weakened by a decade-long period of public debate'. This means the Catholic Church was not united and was weakened by arguments over reform of the Church. The Catholic Church was therefore not ready to take on the challenge of the radical Protestants.

Thirdly, the Scots were wary of the Catholic French and felt it was safer to have English Protestant allies. This is supported in the source by, 'Critical in gaining support towards Reformation was the Protestant English being viewed as allies'.

However, the source only gives some reasons for the Reformation in Scotland. It does not mention important reasons such as the return of John Knox to Scotland. As he moved around Scotland preaching he gathered support wherever he went.

Another important reason was the growth in popular support for reformation among ordinary Scots, even without leaders to inspire them. The Perth riots of 1559 showed how angry people were with the Catholic Church. The people were also burdened by taxation under Mary of Guise and did not like her support for French policies. Furthermore, the Beggars Summons showed how many people thought the poor should be helped more and that friars should not be so greedy and ungodly. Some people even supported Knox and Protestantism because they did not like being ruled by a female. Knox said it was against nature!

The French represented Catholicism and when fighting broke out between French soldiers and ordinary Scots, because the French were a Catholic people, so many Scots saw Catholicism as a bad thing.

Finally there was a lot of Protestant propaganda in the form of plays, songs and literature that gained a lot of popular support for the Reformation.

Why is this a much better answer, and how would it be marked?
The answer to that should be obvious!

1. A judgement is clearly made that the source only partly gives us reasons for support for the Reformation of 1560 in Scotland.
2. The answer includes three points from the source that are explained and supported with source extract evidence.
3. The answer then goes on to provide **seven** other reasons for the growing support for Protestantism. The information is accurate and relevant and linked to the question.

This will get full marks: **9 out of 9 marks**.

Sections 2 & 3 of the Higher History Exam

Sections 2 & 3 overview

Although the content of Section 2 (British History) is different from the content of Section 3 (European and World History) the skills needed to write successful extended responses are the same. As a result Sections 2 & 3 are combined in this chapter.

How do I make sure I answer the question properly?

Any extended response question has two parts – the **topic** and the **task**. The topic is what you will see first when you open your exam paper and look at the questions quickly. You will be asking yourself what the extended responses are about. Do you know information about this topic? Your next thought must be what you have to **do** with your information:

- Are you sure you understand what the question wants you to do?
- How do you make your information **relevant** to the question?

Candidates who score highly in the exam do so because they read the question in the exam paper and then answer that question, not the one they practised weeks or months before.

Is it enough simply to write out as much information as I know?

No, it is not. Extended response writing is about knowing and using detailed information **but** it is even more important to know the process and technique of **how** to write a good extended response. An extended response that simply tells a long story with lots of names, dates and facts will gain you **at most only 6 marks out of 20**.

Why must I have a structure to my extended responses?

The short answer is because you can earn marks for having a structure. Think about the following when planning your structure:

- You will be asked to use information and your own thoughts to argue your case, so your answer must be structured with a beginning, a middle and an end.
- Your answer must be relevant to the question. You will never see a question that asks, 'write all you know about ...'.
- You could be asked whether you agree with an opinion or not.
- You might be asked to explain why certain things happened.
- You might be asked to judge whether something was a success or failure.
- All these types of questions require you to answer in a thoughtful, structured way.

How is my extended response marked?

Although the extended response is out of **20 marks**, those marks are divided into six sections:

- **There are up to 2 marks for an introduction**
- **There are up to 6 marks for accurate and relevant knowledge**
- **There are up to 4 marks for basic analysis comments**
- **There are up to 2 more marks for developed analysis**
- **There are up to 4 marks for evaluating**
- **There are up to 2 marks for a conclusion.**

Structure – the introduction

An introduction is where your extended response starts to take shape, or starts to struggle. Without an introduction there will be no structure because you have not thought **how** you intend to answer the question. If your ideas are not sorted out before you write your introduction, your extended response will decline into storytelling, gaining you at best a C award. The introduction is where you must do your hardest thinking about the topic, what you must do and what will be the main stages of your answer.

How do I write a good introduction?

To get **2 marks** you must have a context, a line of argument and factors to develop.

Context
Context means setting the scene about the question. If you had a question about why attitudes changed towards immigrants in the USA in the 1920s, your context would describe how almost all Americans in 1920 were descended from immigrants who had arrived in the USA in the 19th century, but that the type of immigrant – where they came from and how they were different from other immigrants – changed in the years just before 1918.

In a question about the Liberal Reforms, you would describe why poverty was such a big problem in Britain in the late 19th century, what the policy of laissez faire was and why it did so little to help the poor. In both those cases you will see that contexts make no attempt to answer the question, but they do show that you understand what the topic is about and allow you to then move on to answer the question that has been set.

Line of argument
This means the main argument you will use in your answer. You can write it in a single sentence. The usual way of doing this is to read the question again, spot the main focus of the question (the 'isolated factor') that you are being asked about, then write that the isolated factor was one of the main reasons for something happening, but that there were also other reasons.

The question will usually provide the isolated factor. That means it asks you how important a certain idea was or to what extent that idea explains why something happened. An example would be, 'To what extent were the reports of Booth and Rowntree the main reason why the Liberals introduced reforms to help the poor between 1906 and 1914?'

To answer this question you take the isolated factor of the question – the reports of Booth and Rowntree – and write this, 'The reports of Booth and Rowntree were partly the cause of the Liberal reforms but there were other reasons that influenced the government'. That is all you need. That is your line of argument.

Here is another example:
Question: 'How important was the use of propaganda in the Nazi maintenance of power between 1933 and 1939?'

49

Answer: 'Propaganda was partly responsible for the Nazis maintaining power in Germany but there were other reasons too'.

In both of the examples above the important word is **partly**. Using that word shows you will write about the main idea (the isolated factor) in the question, but that you will also write about other reasons to explain the topic of the question.

Factors to develop
This means the main things you are going to write about other than the isolated factor. For example, for the Liberal reforms question you would follow up your line of argument by writing:

A *Apart from the reports of Booth and Rowntree there were several other reasons that influenced the Liberal government in creating reforms to help the poor. These other reasons included fears over national security and national efficiency, worries about political competition from the new Labour Party, the example of municipal socialism and the arrival into the cabinet of Liberal politicians with new ideas, called the New Liberals.*

By doing this you have shown the marker what you intend to write about but more importantly you have shown yourself what will be in your essay. Each of the points made will become a separate paragraph so now you have planned how your essay will develop.

What do good introductions look like?

Now look at some examples of whole introductions – some good, some not so good. The purpose of this section is to understand why some are good or not so good.

Here is a very weak introduction to an answer to the question, 'To what extent did the Liberals hope to win political advantage by starting a programme of social reforms after 1906?'

A *In order to answer this question it is necessary to explain why the Liberal reforms happened and decide if political advantage was a main reason. The Liberal Reforms began in 1906 and were passed to help the old, the young, the sick and the unemployed.*

Why is this a very weak introduction?

1. It is far too short – only two sentences long.
2. This introduction does nothing to help the writer. Time is wasted by almost writing out the question again. All it does is pretend to be an introduction.
3. There is no context or line of argument. The latter half of the second sentence, which looks like it might be factors to develop, is not relevant to the question that is about **why** the reforms happened.

This introduction scores 0/2.

Here is a better, but still not very good introduction:

There were many reasons why the Liberal reforms were passed after 1906. Political advantage was one reason but so were the effects of reports on poverty from Rowntree and Booth. Rowntree was a York businessman and Booth was a London one and they both found out that almost 30% of the population in their cities lived in poverty. The Liberals were also worried about national efficiency and national security. There were also new ideas about what the Liberal Party should do to help people too poor to help themselves.

Why is this better but not very good?

1. There is no context.
2. The writer understands that the question is about why the reforms were passed but the factors to develop are listed in a very basic way.
3. There is also extra information developing the point about poverty reports that is not appropriate in an introduction.
4. However this introduction does enough to get 1 mark.

Here is a much better introduction:

A *Poverty was a huge social problem in the early 20ᵗʰ century and laissez faire policies were doing little to help. The new Labour Party promised social reforms to help the poor so the Liberal reforms were therefore partly a response to a fear of losing votes to Labour. (1) Other factors also played a part. The reports of Booth and Rowntree proved that one-third of Britain's population lived in poverty. (2)*

The spread of municipal socialism (3) inspired some Liberals to attempt social reform on a national scale. The Liberals were also concerned about Britain's industrial and military power. (4/5) Finally new attitudes in the Liberal Party, called New Liberalism, caused the Liberals to move away from the laissez faire ideology. (6)

Why is this a better introduction?
There is a clear context, a line of argument and several factors to develop. There is no irrelevance and it is clear to a marker you have understood the question.

Why are there numbers in this introduction?
If it helps, there is no reason why you cannot number your separate factors to develop with a pencil as a guide to yourself about what the main paragraphs in the essay will discuss. Such a technique provides a structure that you could follow through the rest of the exam.

Further introduction techniques

Here is another reminder about introduction techniques, this time from a question in the 'Appeasement and the Road to War, 1919–39' topic.
Question: How successfully did Germany pursue its foreign policy between 1933 and March 1938?

Remember, in a 'how successful' answer you must make clear what the success is being judged against. That means you must show what Hitler wanted to achieve, then look at what he did and finally judge whether he achieved his aims.

German foreign policy between 1933 and 1938 was largely based around Hitler's aims outlined in Mein Kampf. His first aim was to destroy the terms of the Treaty of Versailles. (1) His second was to create a Greater Germany including all German-speaking peoples. (2) Another Nazi aim was to achieve Lebensraum for Germany and that was to be found in Russia and Eastern Europe. (3) Finally Nazi ideology was racist and within his foreign policy Hitler wanted to establish the power of the Aryan master race over the inferior peoples of Eastern Europe. (4)

The numbered sentences indicate the signposted points in the introduction that can be expanded into one paragraph for each point. This introduction is now ready to develop with detailed knowledge, analysis and evaluation.

Is the introduction so important – it is only worth 2 marks?

Yes! Although your extended response is out of 20 there are 4 marks that are crucial to your future success. 10 marks out of 20 will gain you a basic C pass. 14 out of 20 will gain you an A pass. It's true! A basic C pass is 50%. An A pass is 70%. Because extended responses are out of 20, multiply your extended response by 5 to see what grade it would gain: 5 × 14 is 70.

Therefore a good introduction can lift your answer by a whole grade and when we move on to look at conclusions (also worth 2 marks) then together the intro and conclusion marks can make the difference between a basic pass at C and an A pass!

Structure – the conclusion

The conclusion is worth **2 marks**. You will get only 1 mark if you simply summarise your essay and make no attempt to weigh up the reasons or factors that together go towards answering the main question.

You will however get 2 marks if you make an overall direct answer to the main question and refer to your factors to develop and the line of argument that you outlined in your introduction. If it sounds a bit complicated, here is a suggestion of a straightforward way to gain the marks.

To follow this suggestion you must write at least a four-sentence conclusion:

- You should start your first sentence with, 'In conclusion …' and then write one sentence that makes a general answer to the main question. That shows the conclusion has started.
- Your second sentence should start with, 'On one hand …' . That shows a marker you are about to **organise** similar points of view and that your answer will be **balanced**. Your information should support one point of view about the extended response title.
- Your third sentence completes the summary and the balance by writing, 'On the other hand …' and here you must sum up the evidence that gives a different point of view about the main question.
- Finally, your fourth sentence should start with, 'Overall …' and then go on to give an overall answer to the main question, perhaps including what you think is the most important point made, the one that led you to your final overall answer.

You can of course write more than four sentences but your total conclusion must have the four parts described here.

Conclusion examples

Here are a couple of examples to show how the process works. The first model conclusion is in answer to the question, 'To what extent had Britain become more democratic by 1918?' Breaking it down, we have:

A
- *In conclusion, Britain did become more democratic between 1867 and 1918 but was not yet fully a democracy.*
- *On one hand, more people gained the right to vote, the system became fairer, there was more choice and people had access to information to make informed choices.*
- *On the other hand, women did not yet have full political equality with men. There was still some plural voting and the House of Lords was still unelected.*
- *Overall, Britain was much more democratic than it had been in 1867 but still had some way to go, including even reforming the UK 'first past the post' voting system, which still raises criticisms today.*

Here is another example of a conclusion in answer to the question, 'To what extent were the Liberal Reforms the result of the growing political challenge from the Labour Party?':

- *In conclusion, the Liberal Reforms were the result of many influences.*
- *On one hand, the political threat from the Labour Party was an important reason for reform but so were concerns about national security and efficiency and the model of municipal socialism.*
- *On the other hand, without the reports of Booth and Rowntree, perhaps awareness of the size of the problem would not have been accepted and would have provided hard evidence for the New Liberalism to push through their ideas about state intervention.*
- *Overall, the Liberals realised that poverty and its causes among the deserving poor could and should be tackled because of many different reasons, but without the political will of New Liberalism perhaps not much would have been done.*

Remember, you can use this structure for almost any essay asked.

Knowledge marks

There are **6 marks** available for using relevant, accurate knowledge in your extended response. These should be easy marks to get. All you have to do is know some detailed facts relevant to the topic you are writing about, but there are some important things to remember about gaining those knowledge marks.

Will I get a mark for each and every correct fact I include in my essay?

No, you will not get marks simply for including 'correct' information. You will, however, get up to 6 marks for using accurate and detailed knowledge, but please note the word 'using'. In the words of the SQA, 'marks can be awarded for evidence which is detailed and which is **used** in support of a viewpoint or factor'. For knowledge marks to be awarded, points must be:

- **relevant** to the issue in the question
- **developed** (by providing additional detail, exemplification, reasons or evidence)
- **used** in a way that links clearly to the question (i.e. explain, analyse).

In other words, it is up to you to show why that information is relevant to the question you are answering. For example, in a question about the various reasons why women gained the vote, if you write, 'The Women's Social and Political Union was formed in 1903 and became known as the Suffragettes' you will have written correct information but it is possible you will get no marks. The reason why you will not get a knowledge mark is because you have not **used** your information by linking it in to the question. Always remember to make clear why you have included some information. What point are you leading up to making? In the example above, you could use the information by writing, 'The Women's Social and Political Union was formed in 1903. The WSPU, known as the Suffragettes, used extreme actions to gain publicity for the cause of votes for women'.

Examples – how to maximise knowledge marks

Look at the following examples. You will see six correct facts about popular topics at Higher. On their own they would probably not gain a mark, but we will see in the table below how they can be developed to guarantee a mark. The important point is to use **relevant information** that **links clearly** to the question.

Topic	Question	Basic knowledge	Knowledge worthy of marks
Germany	To what extent was propaganda the main reason for the rise of the Nazis?	Josef Goebbels was minister of propaganda.	Josef Goebbels was minister of propaganda and he was the mastermind who used posters, film and rallies to win popularity for the Nazis.

Topic	Question	Basic knowledge	Knowledge worthy of marks
Britain	How successfully did the Labour Government of 1945–51 deal with the social problems facing the British people?	The Beveridge Report was published in 1942.	The Beveridge Report was published in 1942 and provided the blueprint that Labour followed in setting up the Welfare State.
USA	To what extent was the growth of the Civil Rights movement in the USA after 1945 due to the emergence of effective black leaders?	In 1954 the Supreme Court ruled that segregation in schools was not constitutional.	The 1954 Supreme Court ruling removed a major obstacle to the growth of civil rights.
Appeasement	How successfully did Britain's foreign policy contain fascist aggression between 1935 and March 1938?	The Spanish Civil War started in 1936 and lasted until 1939.	After the Spanish Civil War broke out in 1936, Britain and France helped form the Non Intervention Committee.

Analysis and evaluation marks

In total there are **10 marks** for this part of your answer, meaning that **half of your marks** in each extended response come from your analysis and evaluation.

What do I have to do to get 4 marks for analysis?

You will get **4 marks** if you made **basic comments** about the information you have included, which shows how the information helps to explain or develop the factor you are writing about. At this basic but effective level, after you have included some factual detail you could write, 'This is important to the question because ...'. That way you cannot avoid using your knowledge to make a judgement about the information.

For example if a question asked, 'To what extent was propaganda important to the Nazi control of Germany after 1933', and you write a simple comment that, 'Propaganda such as rallies at Nuremberg was important because it was watched by thousands of Germans and they were pleased to feel proud of their country again', that would be a basic comment about propaganda. You mentioned rallies and you used the word 'because' to give a reason why they were important. By doing this you will have made a basic analysis comment. If you do this sort of comment at least **four times** in your essay you will gain **4 marks**.

Remember, the easy way to do this is to include a fact or an idea or an event and explain why it was important to the question asked. Your explanation is your analysis.

Examples – how to maximise analysis and evaluation marks

Topic	Question focus	Example answer
USA, 1918–68	Why there was so little progress for civil rights in the 1920s and 30s.	The Ku Klux Klan revived in 1915 and by 1920 it was a very strong organisation, influencing politicians, police and courts. [Fact] This was important in preventing civil rights because many black Americans believed it was pointless to go against such a powerful organisation. [Analysis]
Russia, 1881–1921	Why the Bolsheviks won the civil war.	The White armies were divided and lacked motivation after the death of the Tsar. [Fact] This was important in deciding the outcome of the civil war because the Whites were divided geographically and politically while in contrast the Reds were the opposite, giving them strength to fight for their beliefs. [Analysis]
Britain, 1851–1951	The spread of democracy.	In 1867 Disraeli and the Conservatives passed the Second Reform Act, which increased the number of men given the right to vote. [Fact] The actions of the Conservatives in 'stealing the Liberal's clothes' was important because it gave the vote to many more men and paved the way for more democratic reforms. [Analysis]

Developed analysis

You can get **2 further marks** if you **link your comments directly to the main question**. To follow on from the example above about rallies and propaganda in Nazi Germany, you could write, 'By making Germans feel proud and confident again, the rallies showed that Hitler was keeping his promise of restoring German pride and destroying the hated Treaty of Versailles. These were vital steps in maintaining Nazi control over Germany.' The phrase 'were vital steps in maintaining Nazi control over Germany' is what gains you marks here because you have linked your comments to the main question.

This is developed analysis. You will get one mark for each developed comment and if you do it at least twice in your answer you will get 2 extra marks for analysis, making a total possible of 6 marks for analysis.

Developed analysis examples

Look back at the example above about the Ku Klux Klan. The example ended, '...(they) believed it was pointless to go against such a powerful organisation'. To gain the extra mark you need to link it to the main factor you are writing about, which is the influence of the KKK. Here is the example answer with a more developed analysis that links your point back to the main question:

> **A** *... go against such a powerful organisation because the KKK could either punish people who tried to win civil rights or control politicians into blocking any new laws being made to help civil rights.*

The example from the Russia topic above ended with, 'while in contrast the Reds were the opposite, giving them strength to fight for their beliefs'. You could continue to link this to the main question for an extra mark by writing:

> **A** *This motivation and unity among the Reds was vital to their success, especially as the war continued through long Russian winters.*

The example from the British topic could be improved by writing:

> **A** *The Conservatives believed that extending democracy would result in grateful new voters voting for them, so selfish reasons were as important as idealistic ones in extending the franchise in 19th century Britain.*

The core of this question is about how Labour dealt with the 'Five Giants' identified in the Beveridge Report – namely Want, Squalor, Disease, Idleness and

Ignorance. To gain basic analysis marks on Labour's reforms you might explain the strengths and weaknesses of the Family Allowance Act within a paragraph about Want. Then to gain your extra analysis mark you would explain how important the Family Allowance Act was in the overall campaign against want. For example, was that Act more or less important than the National Assistance Act or Industrial Injuries Act in helping ease the problem of want/poverty?

If you explain the importance of your facts to the factor you are writing about twice, you will get 2 marks for extra analysis. Remember, however, it is always best to give as many examples of this analysis as possible to ensure the marks.

How do I get evaluation marks on top of my analysis marks?

You will get up to **4 marks** for evaluating your information in terms of the question. In other words evaluation is the **judgement** you make about the importance of the main **factors** in terms of the main question. It is not simply commenting on the factual details you include about each individual factor.

To understand that point more clearly look at the diagram below. It shows the main ideas or factors you might use to deal with a question that asked, 'How successfully did the Labour government deal with social problems in Britain during the period 1945–51?'

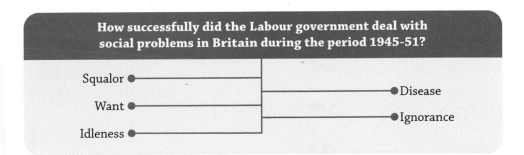

How successfully did the Labour government deal with
social problems in Britain during the period 1945-51?

Squalor

Want

Idleness

Disease

Ignorance

Ways to gain evaluation marks

To achieve evaluation marks you must evaluate the factors in relation to the question. In the example of Labour's welfare reforms, you would argue that the campaign against Want was perhaps more immediately important to the people of Britain than the policy to combat Idleness; or that the creation of the NHS to defeat Disease was more successful than the house building programme to deal with Squalor. Remember the question – it begins, 'How successfully ....', so your arguments must weigh up the success or otherwise of Labour's reforms, based on what Labour aimed to achieve.

If you explain the importance to the question of your main point or factor in comparison to the other main factors **four times** you will get **4 marks** for evaluation. Remember, however, it is always best to give as many examples of this type of evaluation as possible to ensure the marks.

You can also gain marks for evaluation by comparing your factors or the points of view of different historians. For example, think back to the question asked earlier about the importance of propaganda to Nazi control in Germany. In this example you will see that two main factors – propaganda and force – are matched together and an evaluation of their importance is made. If you can suggest that, while propaganda was important, there were other more important ways the Nazis maintained control then that is evaluation of the factors.

You could also weigh up the importance of propaganda by mentioning its negative side, as that suggests it was not such an important reason for keeping control in Germany. For example you could write, 'while propaganda was important in pleasing many Germans and keeping their support, it really only appealed to Nazi supporters. Those people who did not support the Nazis also had to be controlled and for these people *the use of fear and force was more important than propaganda in maintaining control*.' That last part, in italics, is the important evaluation of the factors as opposed to isolated factual detail.

The word 'however' can also be used as a way of gaining evaluation marks. Here is an example dealing with a question about the importance of Bismarck to German unification.

A Economic developments such as the Zollverein certainly helped move the German states towards greater unity, although its influence was economic rather than political. However, Bismarck's influence was political and he had the power of military might and fear of a common enemy to push the states towards his aim of a united German state under Prussian control.

Another route to evaluation, again on Bismarck, could be the use of historians' opinions such as given in this example answer:

While some writers such as Mosse have focused on the importance of Bismarck who, 'did not deal the cards but played his hand well', more recent historical interpretation shows that political changes in Europe and the economic power of the nation state were driving the German states towards greater integration regardless of their fears of Prussianisation.

Summary

Structure is made up of your introduction and conclusion and is worth **4 marks**.

Knowledge is made up of relevant and accurate detail and is worth **6 marks**.

Analysis and Evaluation. Analysis is made up of basic comments worth **4 marks** and developed comments worth an **extra 2 marks**. Evaluation is worth **4 marks**. This makes a total of **10 marks** for this part of your answer.

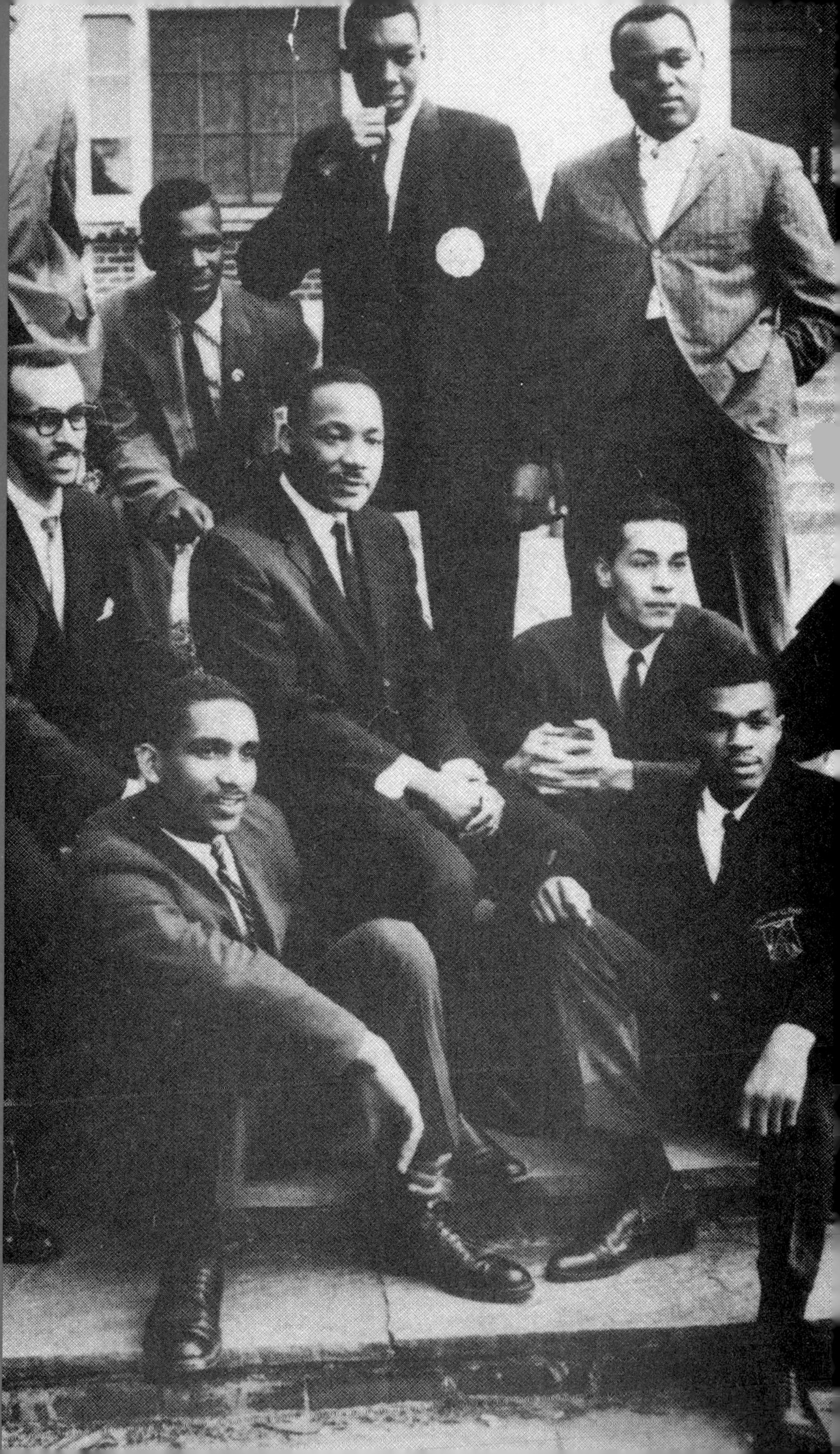

The History Assignment

What is the History Assignment?

At some point during your Higher History course you will be asked to write your History Assignment. The SQA recommends writing the Assignment around March but your teacher/tutor will give you plenty of time to prepare.

Your teachers and the SQA know that you are unlikely to show off your best possible work in an exam that only allows you about 40 minutes to write an extended response. That is why the History Assignment was introduced. It is similar to the National 5 Assignment you probably did last year. By choosing your own title, having time to research and prepare and then one and a half hours to write up your Assignment, you have a chance to show off your best work.

Why is the History Assignment so important?

It is really important to do as well as you can in the History Assignment because the mark you get is part of your final exam mark. In fact, the History Assignment counts for **30 marks out of a total of 90 marks** – Sections 1, 2 and 3 are worth 20 each giving in total the remaining 60 marks.

By doing well in the History Assignment you will have a very useful launch pad for future success. The average mark for History Assignments is just over 18 out of 30 – and that's a B! You can achieve more than that.

How long does my History Assignment have to be?

The answer is simple – what you can write in 90 minutes. That is one and a half hours! There is **no** word limit for the History Assignment. Most people can write one page of A4 in 10 minutes. Since there are 9 × 10 minutes in that 90 minutes then it is quite possible to write a nine-page Assignment and some students write more. The usual length of an Assignment is about six or seven pages long. While it is true that very short Assignments start alarm bells ringing in the heads of markers, given that students have had time to prepare and practice, each Assignment is read and marked on its merits.

Should I try to choose a title that is fresh and new?

No, it's not necessary to choose something that differs from everyone else, and choosing an Assignment title that is deliberately different from any other could cause you problems. Some candidates disadvantage themselves by selecting inappropriate titles for their extended response. Ask your teacher or tutor to check that your title is appropriate.

Are there rules about the title that I can choose?

There is only one rule and that is, your extended response title must be issue based and not simply descriptive. In other words there must be an issue or question within your title such as, '"Appeasement was the only possible policy for Britain to follow when dealing with Nazi Germany." How valid is that opinion?' or, 'How successful was the Labour Government of 1945–51 in dealing with the social problems facing Britain after World War Two?' or, 'To what extent was German unification inevitable with or without Bismarck?'

A good way to check if your extended response is issue based is to look for the question mark at the end. If your extended response has no question mark at the end – such as, 'Appeasement' or, 'The Crusades Fail' or, 'The Tsar, 1917', or, 'Bismarck and the Unification of Germany' then you are likely to get less than half marks. That's because the marker has no way of knowing what you are trying to do apart from simply writing a description of the subject in the title. However, if your title is a definite question, then your extended response should be OK, as it will hopefully answer that original question!

Must I write about something from the syllabus I am studying for the exam?

No, the SQA rules have changed. Until recently your Assignment title had to be part of the syllabus you were studying. That is not now the case. Your Assignment can be about any Historical topic. However, it would be wise to write about a topic you really do know something about and on which you have already had some practice writing well-constructed extended responses.

Are there types of questions to avoid?

Yes, certain styles of questions will cause problems for you and result in fewer marks than you should otherwise get. Beware of the following types of question.

Double questions
Avoid asking two questions in one title. Why give yourself extra work? Bad questions could be:

- 'To what extent was Munich more a success for Hitler or Chamberlain and was it to blame for the outbreak of World War Two a year later?'
- 'Why did the Liberal Reforms happen and how successful were they?'

As a rough guide, avoid the word 'and' in your title because it usually means you are answering two separate questions.

Questions with unclear or unfocussed phrasing
Sometimes your title can make it hard for a marker to know what you are trying to argue, such as:

- 'Was Rowntree the nagging conscience of the Liberals?' (The candidate really wanted to answer a question about the causes of the Liberal Reforms.)
- 'Was Lenin the cork bobbing on the tide of revolution or was he the driving force behind the wave?' This could be asked much more directly as "Lenin was the vital to the success of the Bolshevik revolution in 1917" How valid is that view?'

What types of questions are good styles to choose?

Please notice that the above question contains the word **'styles'**. The following are examples of questions that you could adapt to fit in with your preference for a topic. Look at past papers – there is no reason why you can't choose a past paper question, but check with your teacher or tutor or read this book first. Here is a list of the style of questions that will be used by the SQA when they set questions for your exam. A question that isolates one factor, such as the Britain example below, is a very good style to choose.

- To what extent ...?
- How important ... ?
- How successfully ...?
- How effective ...?
- How valid is this view? – This just means you provide a statement or a quote that gives an opinion such as, 'Bismarck was the man who made German unification possible' and then follow it with, 'How valid is this view?'

Suitable styles of question – examples

From 'The Century of Revolutions, 1603–1702'	'Charles I's attempt to impose his authority in Scotland was a failure.' How valid is this view?
From 'Britain, 1851–1951'	To what extent was the part played by women in the war effort the main reason why some women won the vote in 1918?
From 'Germany, 1815–1939'	To what extent were cultural factors important to the growth of national feeling in Germany between 1815 and 1850?
From 'USA, 1918–1968'	How successful was the New Deal in solving the social and economic problems of the USA in the 1930s?
From 'Appeasement and the Road to War, to 1939'	How successfully did Britain contain the spread of fascism between 1935 and March 1938?

Can I write an extended response based on the Section 1 Scottish Topic?

Yes, you can, but remember there might be some disadvantages. For example, you will not have any past extended response titles to give you ideas to choose from. Because there is no extended response question in Section 1 of your exam paper, you will not have the chance of being lucky and seeing your History Assignment title cropping up in the final exam.

What if my History Assignment title appears in the final exam?

You just got lucky! If you choose your History Assignment from 'mainstream titles' it is quite possible your topic, and perhaps even a title similar to your History Assignment, will appear in the final exam. There is **no** restriction about answering that question based on the knowledge you gained, or indeed from your memory of the structure you used and the analysis points you made. But be careful to adapt your information to fit the **exact question** asked in the exam.

Can I use the same title as my friend?

Yes you can, but before you do, think carefully. It might be a better idea to do a similar question but focus on a different isolated factor in the question. Is your whole class using the same title? That might not be a good idea. The SQA is concerned about lots of Assignments coming from the same school or college with the same titles. Such patterns can result from students choosing a title that has been the subject of a class lesson on how to write an Assignment. That approach can help weaker candidates gain confidence by providing a structure to their extended response, but if you have ambitions to do well then it is always best to do your own work, based of course on advice from your teachers and your experience from doing extended responses that use the same style and structure in writing your answer.

What is the History Resource Sheet?

The History Resource Sheet is used to support you when writing your Assignment. The resource sheet shows markers that you have researched, selected and organised information. It gives you a chance to lay out your Assignment in a rough format that outlines the main stages in your extended response and includes important factual information and ideas. Your History Assignment's History Resource Sheet must be sent to the SQA with your finished extended response.

Are there any rules about the History Resource Sheet?

There are two rules about writing your Assignment. The first rule is that it must be written on one side of A4 paper. In the past there was a word limit of 200 words. That is no longer the case. You can write as much as you want as long as it fits onto one side of A4. You can also word process and print your Resource Sheet information. The same rules then apply.

The second rule is that you must not copy sections of text from the Resource Sheet onto your Assignment. That does not mean phrases and words. It does means you cannot write out sections of your Assignment on your Resource Sheet and then copy them over during the final write-up session. The exception to that rule is the source extracts and resource references you intend to use in your Assignment. They are part of your research for your assignment and must be used in the Assignment. You do not have to memorise them!

How should I organise my History Resource Sheet?

The first thing to do is to make sure that your History Resource Sheet helps you to get as many marks as possible. You should use the History Resource Sheet to organise the information and the source evidence that you will use in your Assignment. To do so you must be clear what your Assignment needs to include.

The History Resource Sheet may include anything you want to use in your Assignment. That could include evidence, data or statistics you have collected from your research. Your information can be organised as bullet points, headings or mind maps. You can have notes and quotes from sources you have used and that could mean details of internet search results, extracts from books or notes taken from a visit or a talk. In fact you can include notes from any source you have used, whether it is from a book, a web site, an interview or a TV programme. You can also organise your resource sheet using lines, boxes and colour. The only thing you cannot do is to prepare your Assignment by writing parts of it out and then copying the same text into your Assignment.

Source evidence

Your History Resource Sheet must also contain source evidence that you will use to support your argument in your Assignment. History is not just names and dates. It is about different points of view about past events. That is called historical interpretations, and historians make careers by arguing with other historians over their interpretation of the past, such as why things happened or what the results were. Including quotes to support your ideas can also help (remember to credit those quotes with the author's name.) But beware! Avoid using trivial 'quotes' to create a bogus impression of real research. For example, 'World War I broke out in 1914' (A.J.P. Taylor). Any quotes you use should express the point of view of the author and if possible be contrasted with a differing point from another source. A further word of warning: 'invented' or 'made up' quotes usually stick out like sore thumbs. They are easily spotted! Finally, remember that there are no extra marks for including a quote, no matter how good it is!

Is the History Resource Sheet really a plan for your assignment?

No, your Resource Sheet is not an exact plan in that you cannot copy out large parts of your Assignment as a rehearsal, and then copy it across into your final Assignment when you are writing it under exam conditions. However, most candidates alter their History Resource Sheet several times before the final 'write-up session'. It is always a good idea to find time to practice writing your Assignment with only the History Resource Sheet to help you. This is an important piece of work, worth 30% of your final grade, so it is important to get the Assignment as near to perfect as you can.

A few people write their Assignment 'fresh' in the exam room, using their History Resource Sheet as help. That means they have not written the full Assignment before. However, most people have practised writing their History Assignment several times before they write the real Assignment in exam conditions. By doing that you have several advantages. First of all, you allow yourself a chance to rethink and edit your work. You can choose to type or hand write at this stage. Word processed (typed) work is easier to change by cutting and pasting, spell checking and so on, but hand writing is good practice for the time you will have in the exam and also, by rewriting over again, you will establish your assignment in your memory.

You might also be able to show your History Resource Sheet to your teachers and tutors for them to offer advice, although they are not obliged to do so and there are strict rules given by the SQA about the amount of help teachers and tutors can give you. The most important thing about your History Resource Sheet is that it should help you to write the best possible Assignment you can.

Will my Resource Sheet be marked?

No it won't, but it may help a marker to understand a point you are making, or it might help them to understand where you intended your argument to go if for any reason you did not finish the Assignment.

Summary

The History Assignment can get you a total of **30 marks** but those marks are made up of lots of smaller marks that you get for doing particular things in your Assignment. Therefore, make sure you follow these golden rules:

1. **Introduction.** Set the context (background) for your issue. To get **3 marks** you must include a line of argument, at least three factors to develop and have two fact points in your context.

2. **Knowledge**. You can get **8 marks** for detailed, accurate and relevant knowledge.

3. **Analysis.** Make clear what the different causes of an event or change were **or** make clear what the main effects of the event or change were. If you have drawn a mind map with the issue at the centre, then the main headings surrounding the main question are what you write about here. Why were they important? How did they help cause the event or change? Why did the change or event lead to the effects you are describing? This is worth **8 marks**.

4. **Evaluation.** From all the causes or effects you have written about, which were more important than others and why? This is really your line of argument. You will get a maximum of **4 marks** for this.

5. **Sources**. Remember to refer to the sources you have chosen to use in your argument. You can quote from them, but remember to also include who wrote

or said your source and where you got this information. To be safe, make a note of the title of the book, article or programme you used, and the name of the author. You will get up to **4 marks** for using four sources in your assignment.

6. **Conclusion** Finally, you should reach a **conclusion** that summarises the different points of view about your question, and then make an overall judgement that directly answers the question you asked at the beginning. This is worth **3 marks**.

Finally, a word about language and style. The SQA gives explicit advice: 'Candidates should not use informal casual style such as, "In this extended response I hope to ..." or, "In my conclusion I have shown that ...". At Higher level a more formal and mature style of writing is expected.' In other words, try not to use these phrases or phrases like them. Try to write in a clear and adult style avoiding slang terms, vague generalisations or text language.

To summarise, if your assignment takes an issue, includes accurate and relevant facts, and looks at different viewpoints and differing interpretations of what happened, and why it happened, before reaching a conclusion, then you are likely to do well.